All Saints' Landbeach

The story of a fen-edge church

Ray Gambell

First Published in 2009 by Milton Contact Ltd.

A CIP catalogue record for this book is available from the British Library.

ISBN 978-0-9562649-2-3

Printed in UK

Milton Contact Limited
3 Hall End, Milton
Cambridge CB24 6AQ
United Kingdom
Order online at *www.miltoncontact.com*

CONTENTS

Acknowledgements

This book is a revised and much expanded version of the author's earlier illustrated description of All Saints' Church in Landbeach (Gambell, 2005). I should like to thank all those people who helped me find and made available reference material, and especially for the many helpful discussions and assistance I received in researching the historic information concerning All Saints' Church. In particular I thank the staff of the Cambridgeshire Archives (formerly the Cambridgeshire County Record Office); Gill Cannell, Sub Librarian of the Parker Library, and Elizabeth Leedham-Green, Ancient Archivist, Corpus Christi College, Cambridge; Frances Willmoth, Archivist of Jesus College, Cambridge; Peter Meadows, Keeper of the Ely Dean & Chapter Archives, and the staff of the Manuscript and Rare Book Departments of the Cambridge University Library; Chloë Cockerill of the Churches Conservation Trust for information on heraldry and Royal Arms; Robert Osborne in Landbeach for help with heraldry; Jim Seaton of Wimborne Minster; and Kate Heard, when at Ely Stained Glass Museum.

I also acknowledge the enthusiasm for our village church, its architecture and contents so freely shared by the late Dr Jack Ravensdale, one time friend and neighbour, and Churchwarden of All Saints' Church from 1971 to 1988.

Finally, I record my appreciation for all the help and advice, particularly concerning photography, received from Chris Thomas in the completion of this book.

ILLUSTRATIONS

ILLUSTRATIONS

ILLUSTRATIONS

All photographs by the author and Christopher Thomas, unless otherwise credited.

PREFACE

The history of the mediaeval parish church of All Saints' in Landbeach is surprisingly well documented. This is a small fen-edge village, but the Rectors were for long the Masters or Fellows of Corpus Christi College in Cambridge, the Patrons since 1359. This means that many of the records of the church have been preserved. The notes made by the College historian, the Revd Robert Masters (Rector 1756 - 1797) are held in the archives of the College and record the alterations he carried out, as well as the furnishing of the church with woodwork he obtained from Jesus College, Cambridge in 1787. The Revd Bryan Walker (Rector 1871 - 1887) described and published the discoveries he made when he carried out an archaeological investigation in 1878 as part of a major restoration. Thus the story of the church over the centuries is reflected in the furnishings and fittings still evident, including the pews, nave roof, windows, angel lectern, tomb slabs, bells, organ and churchyard, as well as some of those which have been removed elsewhere such as the royal coats of arms and the north door.

INTRODUCTION

The village of Landbeach is situated on the edge of the East Anglian fens, 5 miles north of Cambridge on the road to Ely, which is a further 11 miles. The first written references to the village appear in the *Liber Eliensis* dating from about 950 AD. This 'Book of Ely' written by Thomas, a monk of Ely, records that two residents of Beche (the early name for Landbeach/Waterbeach), Oswi and Oscytel (and Sexferth the father of Oscytel) were amongst the twelve thanes of Cambridgeshire who acted as witnesses to the transfer of lands and property in the district (Fairweather, 2005). It is probable that there was a Saxon church in the village at this time, but although Utbeche (Landbeach) is mentioned in the Domesday Book of 1086 (Domesday Book, 2002), churches were not generally listed in that compilation of land.

Utbeche was the Beche out of the water, to distinguish it from Waterbeach, which was much prone to flooding being close to the River Cam (Ravensdale, 1974). Villagers from the latter settlement took their animals to pasture on the higher ground at times of inundation and so established what became a separate permanent habitation in the Saxon period. The river Cam was still tidal as far as Waterbeach at this time. (Rawle, 2005).

The parish church of All Saints' in Landbeach stands out from the flat fen-edge landscape and can be seen across the fields from miles around. This is particularly the case at night when the tower and spire are bathed in a golden hue (Frontpiece). The floodlighting was installed in the year 2000 AD with money raised by the village people to mark the start of the new millennium.

The lights are a fitting embellishment and tribute to the Grade I listed building that has been the centre of Christian worship and community life in the village for some 900 years. The church is, as in many small villages in East Anglia, the oldest building in Landbeach.

We are fortunate that the history of the church has been well documented by a number of authors. The Revd Robert Masters, who was Rector of Landbeach from 1756 to 1798, made major alterations to the building when he came to live in the Rectory next door. He introduced a great deal of woodwork from Jesus College, Cambridge, and the east window, and left extensive records in his notebooks of his activities. The Revd William Keatinge Clay wrote an important history of Landbeach in 1861, as well as the histories of other local villages. The Revd Bryan Walker, Rector 1871 - 1887, published the results of the major archaeological investigations he carried out in the church and the numerous changes he introduced in 1878. The Revd Ronald Kynaston Denham, Rector 1922 – 1948, printed material in the Landbeach parish magazine over several years gathered from Walker's notes. Many of the original early records of the church are also preserved, due particularly to the association with our Patrons from the mid 14th century, Corpus Christi College, Cambridge, who usually nominated the Master or a Fellow as Rector from that time. The Parish Registers, recording the baptisms, marriages and burials, were first ordered to be kept in the Church of England by Thomas Cromwell in September 1538. The Landbeach Registers begin the following month and are virtually continuous thereafter (Cambridgeshire Archives, 2004).

The connection between Corpus Christi College and the church had a long gestation. William the Conqueror controlled the district around Ely after subduing the resistance put up by Hereward and his followers. William then granted the lands formerly belonging to the Abbey of Ely to Picot, the Norman sheriff of Cambridgeshire, while land previously belonging to King Edward went to two cartwrights – thus establishing the two manors in Landbeach comprising some 660 and 550 acres of land respectively. For long known as the Manors of Chamberlaynes and Bray, they are now represented by Manor Farm and Worts Farm. Picot may have built the second church in Landbeach, although he did not live here but in Cambridge or Bourne, one of his other manors. He let out his Landbeach property to a tenant named Muccullus. Picot's son, Robert, inherited the manor but was banished by Henry I in 1106 for siding against the king with the king's brother Robert, Duke of Normandy. The property was forfeited and given to a cousin, Payne de Peverel. This family were lords of the manor for two generations. Payne died of a fever in London about 1122 and his only son William went on a Crusade and died in Jerusalem.

The Manor then passed by the marriage of one of the latter's sisters, Alice, to Hamon de Peche who was sheriff of Cambridgeshire and Huntingdonshire in 1164. It remained with the family of de Peche until the 1300s. They did not occupy the Manor but sub-let it, a practice known as subinfeudation, so that they did not have to pay the king a large fee for selling it outright. The first family in this tenancy were called de Beche, obviously because of where they lived in Beach or Landbeach. They occupied the manor house whose remains can be seen in the undulations of the moat and fishponds to the east of the church.

Aleyn de Beche presented the first Rector we know by name, Pers de Cantebrigg, about 1160 in the reign of Henry II. Around 1240 the property went to Aleyn's daughter Helen de Beche, who married Geoffrey le Bere d'Elyngtone and went away to live with her husband. So she subinfeudated her property to Sir Walter Chamberlayne. Sir Walter became perpetual tenant in 1250, and in 1290 a law was passed ending any further subinfeudation. At first the Chamberlaynes had to pay the Beres 2 shillings a year rent, but this was later remitted provided they gave the Beres a rosebud regularly on St John's Day, 24 June. The Chamberlaynes retained this Manor and the patronage of the church for just over a century. Thebaud le Chamberlayne was Rector about 1255, presented by his father Sir Walter, and John le Chamberlayne was Rector 1294 - 1299, presented by his father, also Walter, grandson of Sir Walter. Finally, Sir Thomas le Chamberlayne, the fifth and last of the family, sold the manor to Corpus Christi College in 1359. However, it was several more years before the College recovered all the small claims on the right of presentation and on the Manor itself that had accreted from earlier generations and families (Clay, 1861).

The church was named All Saints at least by 1439 when Johannes Swayne of Landbeach, who died on 14 May of that year, made a benefaction of an acre of land for the maintenance of *ecclesie omnium sanctorum* (Clay, 1861).

Dr J R Ravensdale (1986), a historian and resident in the village for many years, described the setting of the village and its history, and outlined the development of the church building. Barges would have carried stone for the church from the Northamptonshire limestone quarries, and later the softer Cambridgeshire clunch, along the medieval canal that passes close by to the east of the church. The earliest parts of the building as we see it today, the tower and chancel, date back mainly to the 13th century, probably built by the Chamberlayne family. In the mid 14th century the chancel was extended and the tower was rebuilt. The diagonal French buttresses were probably added to the tower in the later 14th century to strengthen the structure for the addition of the spire. The aisles were widened and the south porch added in the mid 15th century. The clerestory was added about the same time when the nave roof was raised, reusing the 14th century tie beams. The Victorian restoration in 1878 included building the vestry and organ chamber on the site of the former Lady Chapel that was demolished in 1787.

The steeple was repaired, and the spire pointed, in 1745 by a man named Thomas Sumpter (Clay, 1861) and again restored in 1879. Denham (1924b) wrote that the letters 'H. A.' on the wind vane on top of the spire, which is 91 feet [27.7m] from the ground, are the initials of Messrs Hall and Ambrose, Churchwardens at the time. The date on the wind vane is 1865 (Fig. 1).

Electric light was installed in the church in memory of her parents by Mrs Money (Denham, 1936); the lights were dedicated in January 1937. A plaque by the tower records this gift (Fig. 2).

The south aisle was restored in 1980, the north aisle and nave roof in 1983 (Cambs CC, 1985), and the tower and spire in 1985.

A North Porch, providing level disabled access and housing a toilet, sink facility and boiler room, were added in 2006 (Figs. 3 & 4). A new heating system was installed in the church at the same time, with the pipe-work laid under the wood floors beneath the pews as these were lifted and replaced, a procedure necessitated by the rotten state of the floorboards and bearers.

An Ordnance Survey benchmark on the southwest buttress of the tower (Fig. 5) gives a height above mean sea level of 8.07m (26.5ft). The dates of 1813 and 1993 on the South Porch (Fig. 6) reflect repairs carried out at those times to the 15th century structure, which contains a mutilated holy water stoup outside the church door (Fig. 7).

Fig. 1 Wind vane

Fig.2 Plaque recording the installation of electric light

Fig. 3 North Porch

THIS NORTH PORCH WAS
OPENED & DEDICATED
BY THE ARCHDEACON OF
CAMBRIDGE
THE VEN. JOHN BEER
11 FEBRUARY 2007

Fig. 4 North Porch plaque

Fig. 5 Benchmark on tower buttress

Fig 6 South Porch

Fig. 7 Mutilated Holy Water stoup

Fig. 8 Norman stone with chevron marking in west wall

THE EARLY CHURCH

Evidence of an earlier church appeared when some good Norman stonework that had been re-used was discovered during the restoration carried out in the 1980s. A finely cut piece of chevron decoration and a scalloped capital uncovered in the east wall of the chancel *"mean that we must look for a stone church in Landbeach a century or more further back than we did before"* (Ravensdale, 1986). Since then a further chevron-marked stone was revealed in the wall of the south aisle when a piece of the cladding fell off (Gambell, 2005). Chevron inscribed pieces of stone have now also been identified in the west (Fig. 8) and south walls of the tower, so that re-used Norman stone is evident on at least three sides of the building.

A number of carved faces and gargoyles decorating the outside of the building, including the tower, probably date from the medieval period (Fig. 9).

There are shields on the four sides of the tower under the battlements; on the west, a fleur-de-lys; on the south, two keys; and on the east, a cross. Walker (1879a) pointed out that the shield on the north side bears *"the arms of the Guild of Corpus Christi, and not the combination of these arms with those of the Guild of the Virgin which formed the armorial device of the college of Corpus Christi until the Reformation. Hence the tower would seem to have been completed before the college obtained the patronage of Landbeach, i.e. prior to 1359"*.

Walker, based on the archaeological investigations carried out during the course of his restoration of the building (1879a), drew a ground plan of the church as he thought it was about 1450 (Fig. 10). He conjectured that there were two original Guild Chapels in the west ends of the two side aisles; various wills dating from the early 1500s preserved in the Ely Registry make reference to bequests of candles and to pay for prayers to be said in the chapels of the Guild of All Hallows and Jesus. There was also a chapel of St James, which from the position of the piscina in the south aisle, was in the eastern bay of this aisle. A mortuary chapel, no longer evident beyond the present east end of the south aisle, was the burial place in 1345 of Henry Chamberlayne. The Lady Chapel on the north side of the chancel, some four or five feet wider than the north aisle and the same length as the chancel, was still standing in 1757 but removed soon afterwards by Robert Masters. There was also a rood screen across the chancel arch, with a staircase on the south side, and the pulpit on the north side.

The furnishings and decorations described in the following pages illustrate something of the early appearance of the church from its medieval beginnings, and the subsequent alterations and embellishments over the centuries.

Fig. 9 Gargoyles

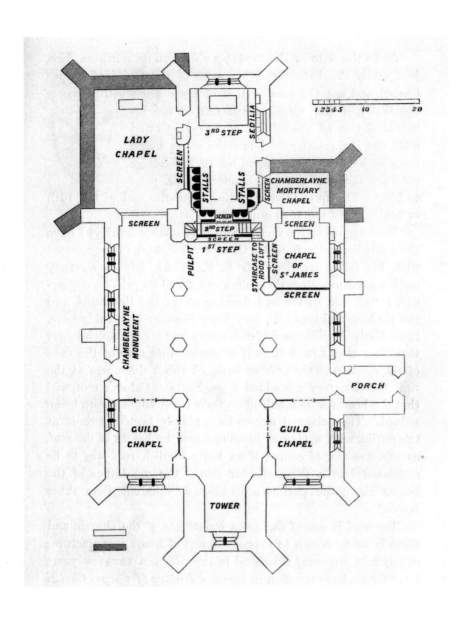

Fig. 10 Floor plan of church in 1450 (from Walker 1879)

EARLY WOODWORK

Evidence of some early woodwork remains in the church. Walker (1879a) believed that *"The stalls, four in number, standing in the Landbeach chancel, obviously did not come from Jesus College. They seem to have formed, with the screen and pulpit, parts of a single composition."* Mr George Wood, one of the church architects, in his notes cited by Walker, commented that *"The original arrangement of the woodwork at the entrance to the chancel we found in situ; it was evidently made for the church, and not adapted, (and probably was coeval with the clerestory windows and the roof as readapted."*

Walker continues: *"As to the four stalls above mentioned, we may note that two of them have under the seats in place of miseres the arms of l'Isle and Arundel, bishops of Ely from 1345 to 1361 and from 1374 to 1388, respectively, who, as far as I know, had nothing to do with Jesus College, or the foundations out of which it sprung; though they might naturally enough be benefactors of a parish as to part of which they were the superior lords."*

Masters himself (1756 - 98) *"thought it probable from these arms that the Bps of Ely Lyle & Arundel were contributors towards erecting those seats."*

Clay (1861) gave an account of these arms: *"In both the rector's pews 'under the screne,' (which existed in 1745, but was subsequently removed by Mr Masters,) are likewise two oaken seats, or stalls, with miseres, the bottoms whereof were once covered with carved shields. Two of these miseres were, in 1745, decorated with the arms of Bishops de L'Isle, and Arundel, the shields having then been removed from the two others: now they have all been removed... The two shields just referred to, emblazoned, are placed on the east end of the chancel with those of the college, and Mr Masters, also on wood."*

Fig. 11 Arms of Thomas de l'Isle on Miserere

Fig. 12 Arms of Bishop Thomas Arundel on Miserere

The two Bishops' shields are now once again on the miseres (Figs. 11 & 12). The de l'Isle arms are two chevrons separated by a horizontal bar: the Arundel arms have two erect lions and chequers in quarters. The two shields for Corpus Christi College and Robert Masters are fixed on the south wall of the chancel, together with another bearing the religious insignia 'IHS' (Fig. 13).

Then in his account of the rectory Clay wrote (1861) *"Hung up in the hall, are three well-executed coats of arms on wood, preserved in all probability for their workmanship, one having the arms of Zouch[1] and of Whitmore[2], quarterly: whilst of the others one bears simply the arms of Zouch... the other the arms of Whitmore..."*

When the Diocese of Ely sold the rectory into private hands in 1977 these three shields were removed. They are now placed on the south wall of the south aisle of the church, with a fourth shield bearing the arms of the Revd Bryan Walker (Fig. 14). The Zouch arms comprise ten roundels and the Whitmore arms interweaving diagonals.

---

1 *The Zouches were the descendants in the female line of the earls of Brittany.*

2 *Sir George Whitmore, Knt. A distinguished native of Shropshire, was closely connected with Waterbeach. See Clay's History of that parish, pp. 76 &c. ["the real benefactor to Waterbeach was Sir George Whitmore, Knt."].*

Corpus Christi College

The Revd Robert Masters

Religious symbol

Fig. 13 Coats of arms on the chancel wall

The Revd Bryan Walker

Zouch Arms

Whitmore Arms

Zouch & Whitmore Arms

Fig.14 Coats of arms on the south wall

CHAMBERLAYNE MONUMENT / EASTER SEPULCHRE

In the north aisle, just east of the North Door, there is an ornately carved stone archway in the north wall (Fig. 15). Clay, (1861) noted that *"Tradition ascribes it to some member of the Chamberlayne family, whose arms can be traced in the adjoining window, argent, 2 bendlets dansetté, sable."* Clay, from one of the two seals attached to Henry le Chamberlayne's will, then identified the arms and thus the monument with Sir Thomas Chamberlayne, the founder of the present church building.

Walker (1871 - 87) wrote, concerning the stained glass in the centre window of the north aisle: *"In the second window of the N. Side near the door and just above the old arched monument in the N aisle is a very old coat of arms, but plaistered over within to save glazing, as are the tops of all the windows, by some saving and thrifty churchwarden. On the outside by help of a ladder I easily made them out, viz. A. two cotises dansse G., and between them white glass to fill up part that was broken but should be a bend as is evident from 2 seals of the arms of Chamberlain in my 8ᵗʰ vol. p. iv and 139. From this circumstance I think it probable that the said old-fashioned monument belongs to one of that family who were long Lords of the Manor here. The field is diapered, as all very old glass used to be: so that the added glass is easily distinguished."*

The description of the arms in the Anglo-French language of heraldry can be interpreted as a blue diagonal stripe between two narrow wavy red lines on a blue or silver background.

Fig. 15 Chamberlyne memorial / Easter sepulchre

Walker later noted (1871 - 87) that: *"The arms of Chamberlayne in the window were repaired in 1880, diapered glass being inserted instead of plain white glass in the bend. At the same time Mr W.H. Constable, artist in glass, Cambridge, gave the arms of Trinity Hall or of the Bateman family to the church. He informed me that they had been originally in a window in Thurlow Church, Essex. These were inserted in the tracery next to the Camberlayne arms."*

These two windows are illustrated in Fig. 16.

The reason for adding the second arms is unclear. A possible connection is that when the Guild of Corpus Christi and the Guild of St Mary jointly founded Corpus Christi College in 1352, William Bateman, Bishop of Norwich, was involved in obtaining a new site for the College. He had already founded Trinity Hall in 1350, and later completed Gonville Hall (Gray & Stubbings, 2000). We may also note that Walker was a former scholar of Trinity Hall.

Fig.16 Arms in north aisle window

Ravensdale (1986) believed strongly that the stone monument in All Saints' Church is in fact a fine example of a common type of Easter Sepulchre, associated with the ritual and ceremonial of the Easter Mass. Part of the evidence for this view comes from pre-Reformation wills of 1504, 1519 and 1530 leaving money to endow the light kept in the Sepulchre during the Easter Vigil (cited in Clay, 1861). At all events, the monument is an interesting piece of carving, including a charming face on the left side (Fig. 17).

Fig.17 Face on Chamberlayne memorial / Easter sepulchre

NAVE ROOF

An outstanding feature and great ornament of the church is the 15th century nave roof. Four carved angels in feathered suits alternate with four robed benefactors to decorate the hammers between the tie beams, each bearing a painted shield. The angels' wings are missing, although their mortises are still evident (Fig. 18).

Fig. 18 Roof angel showing mortise for wing

The roof (Fig. 19) was probably the model for Nicholas Toftys, *"carpenter of Landbeche"* to use in about the year 1450 when he *"entered into an agreement with the cherche revys of St Benedict in Cambridge, for a new roof of their church with ornaments of angels, &c"* (Masters, 1753).

Mrs Fanny Seymour Walker, the wife of the Revd Bryan Walker, repaired the roof shields in 1885 to illustrate something of the history of the parish (Denham, 1925c). Rather than carrying out this work *in situ*, it is probable that Mrs Walker painted the coats of arms on fabric at ground level and then had someone else nail the material in place on the shields.

The roof shields (Fig. 20), in order from the east end, represent the Guild of Corpus Christi and the Guild of the Blessed Virgin Mary (the two Cambridge Guilds that founded Corpus Christi College); the University of Cambridge; Corpus Christi College, our Patrons from 1359; Matthew Parker, Rector of Landbeach 1545-1554, who was appointed Archbishop of Canterbury under Queen Elizabeth I; the Diocese of Ely; the family of the 13th century builder of the present church, the Chamberlayns who were Lords of the Manor next to the church; and the Revd Bryan Walker, the Victorian restorer of the church.

Fig. 19 Nave roof

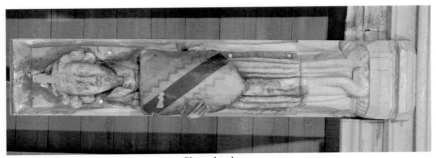

Chamberlayne

Matthew Parker

University of Cambridge

Guild of Corpus Christi

Fig. 20a Nave roof shields – south side

Bryan Walker

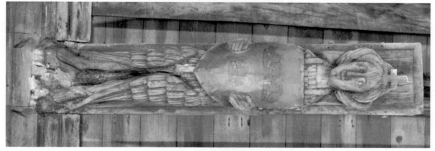

See of Ely

Corpus Christi College, Cambridge

Guild of the Blessed Virgin Mary

Fig. 20b Nave roof shields – north side

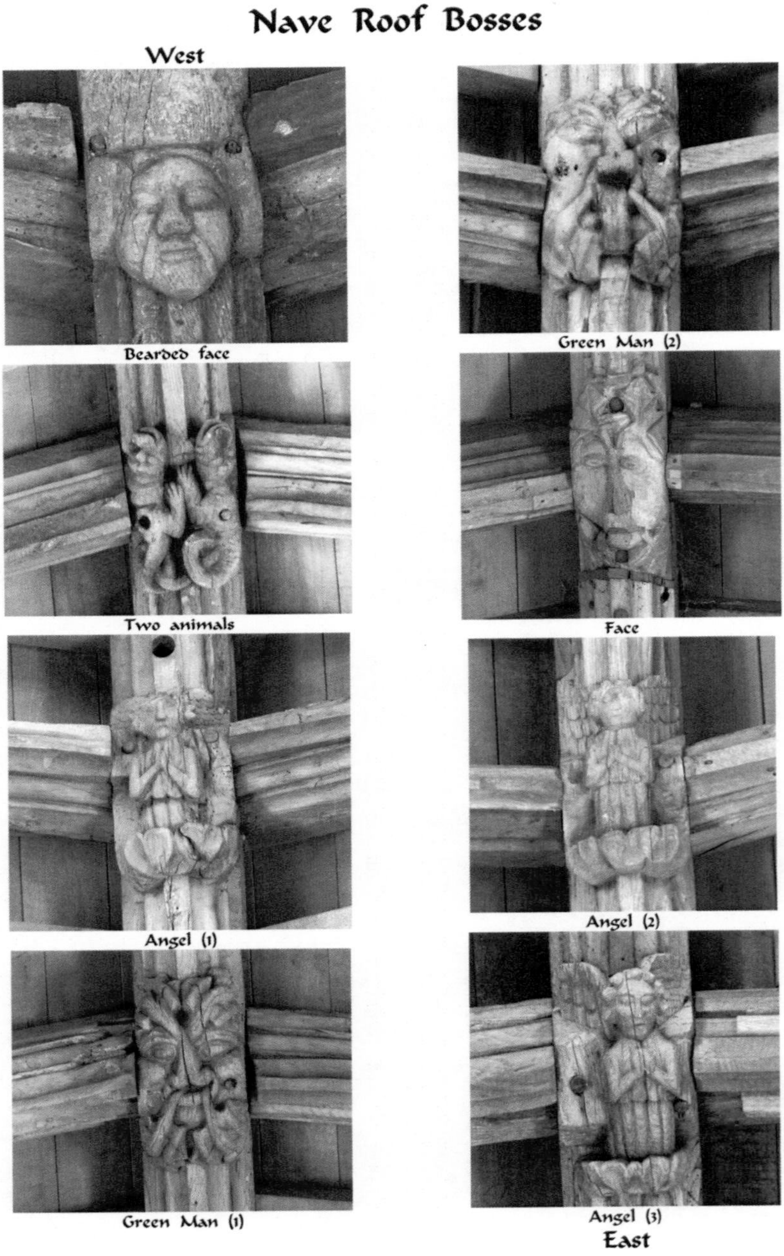

Nave Roof Bosses

West

Bearded face

Green Man (2)

Two animals

Face

Angel (1)

Angel (2)

Green Man (1)

Angel (3)

East

Fig. 21 Nave roof bosses

A series of eight carved wooden bosses along the centre line at the apex of the nave roof include human faces, winged angels, mythical animals and two Green Men (Fig. 21). They exemplify the secret humour and workmanship of their carvers, hidden away as they are in the inaccessible height of the roof.

GREEN MEN

In addition to the two examples on the nave roof already noted above, there are a number of other Green Men to be seen in All Saints'. These pagan fertility symbols, with leaves and other vegetation issuing from their mouths, are a rather surprising but not uncommon feature of the woodcarver and stonemason's craft to be found in many Christian churches. A particularly intriguing example occurs on the tie beams of the nave roof, where there is a transition from a winged angel on the eastern-most beam (Fig. 22) to a full Green Man mask sprouting large lobed leaves from his mouth on the western-most beam (Fig. 23).

Ravensdale (1986) also pointed out that there are three more Green Men carved in wood on the wall plate of the south aisle (Fig. 24). In fact there are four, but one is badly defaced. Two finely carved stone faces appear on either side of the east window on the outside of the church, with luxuriant foliage issuing from the mouths and enveloping the heads (Fig. 25). It is clear that the deeply held old beliefs were still remembered when All Saints' was being built or extended.

Fig. 22 Winged angel on east tie beam in nave roof

Fig. 23 Green Man on west tie beam in nave roof

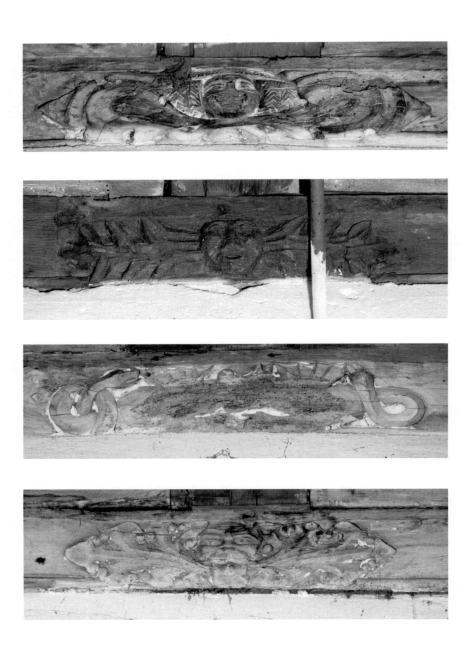

Fig. 24 Green Men on the south aisle wall plate

Fig. 25 Green Men outside east window

NORTH AND SOUTH AISLE CORBELS

There are a number of other interesting carvings decorating the north and south aisle roofs. Clay (1861) remarks that *"The roof of the north aisle is good with its oaken flowers for bosses, and its small angels."* The four bosses are illustrated in Fig. 26. The angels are in fact decorations on the corbels and occur in both aisles. A corbel is a projection from the wall to support the weight of the roof borne by the wall-posts.

There are five of these carvings on each side of each aisle. In the north aisle the carvings are full-length wooden figures in varying poses, six holding shields, two with hands held as in prayer, and two others clasping scrolls or sheaths of some kind (Fig. 27).

In the south aisle the stone angels have wings and hold a variety of objects including six with shields, three with musical instruments - pan pipes, a stringed lute-like instrument and a recorder-like instrument, while one is too mutilated to identify (Fig. 28).

Fig. 26 Flower bosses in north aisle roof

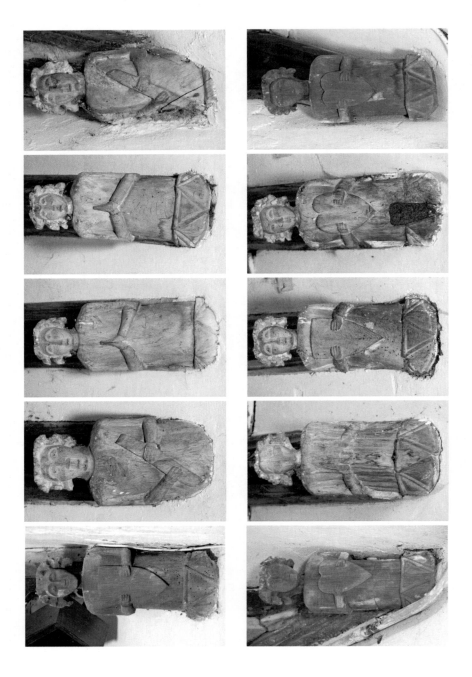

Fig. 27 Corbel figures in the north aisle

Fig. 28 Corbel figures in the south aisle

CHEST

Another of the older pieces of woodwork in the church is the iron-bound chest (Fig. 29). It has a carrying handle at each end, although its great weight must have made it scarcely portable. There are two key holes and locks, and from the style it is dated to about 1500. In the church inventory of 1613 (Clay, 1861) this chest is recorded as *'a great chest barred wth Iron wth ij lockes to keepe the bookes and lynnen.'*

At the time when Clay wrote about the church in Landbeach (1861) this chest, *"a very large oaken chest clamped with iron"*, stood in the west end of the north aisle, which served as a vestry at that time. Following the Victorian restoration some 25 years later the chest was moved to a position in front of the first pew at the east end of the north aisle. More recently it was moved again, to the west end of the south aisle, in the re-ordering of the furniture when the new heating system was installed in 2006.

Fig. 29 Medieval chest

CHALICE

Also recorded in the church inventory of 1613 is a further item of special importance to the present congregation, the Communion Chalice (Fig. 30). This is still in regular use, and was listed in 1613 as '*Imprimis a silver Cvppe wth a Cover damasked for the Communion*'. Clay (1861) goes on to describe the silver cup and cover:

'*This silver cup has on it For the towne of Landbeach. The cup and cover are both beautifully ornamented, and were once very handsome: they are now much worn, and battered. Since they are without any of the usual Assay Office letters, we cannot determine their date. There is only a v within a heart-shaped indentation, and that on the cup, the private mark of the maker, or seller.*'

The exact age of this chalice is uncertain. An inventory of Church Goods made on 4th August 1552 includes '*Plate. Fyrste one chaliyce wth y^e patent of Sylver, poiz. xvj^{oz}*'. It may be that this is the same chalice, but the style of the vessel certainly suggests that it dates from around the Elizabethan period.

Fig. 30 Chalice

BELLS

The tower of Landbeach church contains four bells (Fig. 31). At the time when Clay (1861) wrote, two of them were cracked. These were the treble and second bells, weighing respectively 5½ and 6½ cwt., and both bear the inscription:

JOHN DRAPER MADE ME 1619.

These bells were cast in the foundry at Thetford in Norfolk. Stephen Tonne at Bury St. Edmund's made the third bell in 1577. The inscription to this effect is:

DE BURI SANTI EDMONDI STEFANUS TONNI
ME FECCIT W.L. 1577 FAVET IOVA POPULO SUO.

This bell weighs 8 cwt and later also cracked, and eventually all the bells were restored in 1929. The three bells that had been cracked were recast by Messrs. J. Taylor and Co. of Loughborough, and together with the original tenor bell, were rehung in a new frame. A rough inscription on the wall of the bell chamber records the names of the three local ringers – C. Smith, W.J. Abraham and R.W. Ballard - involved in this work (Fig. 32).

The tenor bell is original, and weighs 11½ cwt. Clay (1861) relates that this bell is supposed to have been cast about 1350, and credited W. Ffounder as the maker, although there is no inscription to this effect. The maker's stamp is of a particularly elaborate form and actually identifies it as cast by William Culverden at Aldgate between 1510 and 1523.

Fig. 31 Landbeach bells from above

Fig. 32 Inscription in bellchamber

The founder's mark was described when the two quarter bells at Hampton Court Palace were cleaned and rehung in 1947 (Anon., 1947). The Landbeach bell is one of only about a dozen of this founder's bells still in existence, and the only one in Cambridgeshire with this mark. The maker's mark on the two Hampton Court Palace bells are almost indistinguishable but it is very clear and prominent on the Landbeach bell. However, it is not easy to see because when the bells were rehung the tenor was turned through 90° so that the mark is now only a foot away from the west wall of the tower.

William Culverden's trademark is in the shape of a shield, the centre of which is occupied by a large bell (Fig. 33). Across this are the letters FOUN of the word *"founder"*. Below on the left is a W and on the right the figure of a bird. Along the top of the shield are the words IN DNO COFIDO, with a trefoil and the letters DE below. Right at the bottom is a mark like two back-to-back Ps.

Fig. 33 Culverden crest on tenor bell

These various signs have been interpreted as follows. Culver is an old English word for pigeon, which presumably is the bird depicted. Combined with the letters W and DE, most of the maker's name, W. Culverden, is then represented. The other letters come from the beginning of the Latin Vulgate Version of Psalm 11: *"In Domino Confido"* – 'In the Lord I put my trust; how say you then to my soul that she should flee as a bird unto the hill.' The other marks are unexplained, but the trefoil may be a reference to the Holy Trinity, and there was a priory of that name close to William Culverden's foundry in Aldgate.

We can note that Culverden's founding interests passed to the Tonne family who began the Bury foundry, which later moved to Thetford under the Draper family. Thus the four Landbeach bells, although made at different dates and in different foundries, all have a family connection in their origin, and now in their belfry.

ROYAL COAT OF ARMS

Another item no longer to be seen in All Saints' is the Royal Coat of Arms (Fig. 34). Clay (1861) in his description of the church wrote:

"The east face of the tower inside the church bears the royal arms. They were fixed there, 16th December, 1826, having been brought from the old hall of the college [Corpus Christi], the gift of the master and fellows. Dr Gunning, afterwards bishop of Ely, had put them up over the hall-table, at an expense of £20 in 1660, the year in which he was made master. The royal arms previously in Landbeach church, and in 1745 hanging over the chancel screen, are in Milton church."

These Arms, now hanging over the High Table in the College Hall, are of a finely carved wooden design mounted on an elaborate frame. The centre shield has the three lions of England in the first and third quarters, and the Scottish Arms introduced by James the First of England and Sixth of Scotland in the second quarter. These comprise a red lion rearing on its hind legs on a gold background, with narrow lines interlaced with fleurs-de-lys pointing alternately inwards and outwards. The Irish harp occupies the second quarter.

In the centre of the shield is a smaller shield, or pretence. This shield is divided into three, the upper half with two gold lions on a red field to the left of a rearing blue lion on a gold background, representing Brunswick and Luneburg. Below is a galloping white horse on a red background, the symbol of Hanover.

Fig. 34 Royal Coat of Arms in Corpus Christi College

Although this design dates from the succession of George, Elector of Hanover to the English throne as George I in 1714, the fact that a crown surmounts the Corpus Christi pretence dates it to 1816 or later when Hanover became a kingdom. It seems possible therefore that the Arms were updated when fixed in Landbeach Church in 1826.

The Revd R.K. Denham (1925b) in his series of articles on the history of the parish and church, pointed out the *"finely carved Royal Arms above the Tower Arch"* and went on to describe their origins. He thought that Dr Peter Gunning probably composed the prayer 'For all sorts and conditions of men' in the 1662 Prayer Book.

Later, Denham (1928) writing in the Landbeach Parish Magazine for March that year announced the following news:

"In accordance with a faculty requested by a majority of the Parochial Church Council, the Royal Arms of King Charles II were returned to Corpus Christi College on March 15 . . The College has a real claim upon the Arms. They were hung in the College in 1660, where they remained until 1826, when they were brought here. No record can be found that they were ever formally given to this parish. In 1660 they cost £20, and for their return the College has now given £100 towards the Bells Fund. Thus the Arms are returning to their original home. A good photograph of them will be hung in the Church to commemorate their sojourn here. The College has also given £20 as a donation to the Bells Fund."

The photographs of the west end of the church taken before 1878 and around 1900 (see below at Figs. 47 upper & 57a) both show the arms on the wall of the tower. Faint markings on the plaster of the west wall of the nave, against the tower, still indicate today where these Royal Arms had once hung. The Commandment Boards visible on either side of the tower arch are still in place (Fig. 35). Such boards were ordered to be set up on the east wall of churches in the reign of the first Queen Elizabeth, and they must have been moved to their present position prior to the Victorian restoration.

Extracts from the churchwardens' accounts from 1639 to 1681 (quoted by Clay, 1861), include the following items relating to the first Royal Arms in the church:

> "*1650   Paid goodman Lawrence*
> *for defacing the kinges armes   £0 2s 0d.*"

> "*1660   Paid to the Painters*
> *for seting up the Kings armes   £2 5s. 0d.*"

Thus were the original Royal Arms in Landbeach treated at the beginning and end of the Commonwealth under Oliver Cromwell.

These original painted Royal Arms now hanging over the south door of All Saints' Church, Milton, are illustrated in Fig. 36. Three of the quarters show the arms of England (three gold lions on a red background), France (three gold fleur-de-lys on a blue background), and Ireland (a gold harp with silver strings on a blue background), while the fourth lower right quarter has the arms of the Hanoverians dating from 1714 to 1801. The monarch's initials lettered at the top are GIIR, George II who reigned from 1727 to 1760, so clearly the arms had been further updated before going to Milton.

Fig. 35 Commandment Boards

Fig. 36 Royal Arms now in Milton Church

JESUS COLLEGE WOODWORK

In his description of the church Clay (1861) commented that even then *"Its ancient wood-work constitutes, in fact, the great recommendation of the church, and renders it so attractive an object to the curious, the whole building, from the east end of the chancel to the tower arch, together with the vestry, being full of it. It was brought from Jesus college chapel in 1787 by Mr Masters. The authorities of that college had disposed of it, because they wished to arrange the interior of their chapel more in accordance with the ideas then prevailing of comfort and neatness".*

The restoration of the Chapel of Jesus College in 1789 - 1792 involved removal of the 16th century stalls from the chancel (Morgan, 1914):

"Some sections of the old carved woodwork were sold to the carpenter who removed them, while others, which included the pulpit and screen, were bought for the sum of five guineas by the Rev. Robert Masters, a member of Corpus College and a well-known antiquary, who was then Rector of Landbeach near Cambridge, and were placed in his church."

The College accounts for 1791 actually include two entries for money received under the heading 'Expense of fitting up the Chapel' (Jesus College, Cambridge, 1791) viz:

"Wood sold to Mr Masters - 3. 3. 0"

"Wood sold to Mr Masters - 2.12.6"

The furnishings of the chancel in Jesus College Chapel in the early 1500s of stained glass and carved wood *"were probably more beautiful and elaborate than any the nuns [of the original foundation] had known. The crest of Bishop Alcock, [the founder of the College] by a play on his name, was a cock triumphant upon a globe, and this was repeatedly displayed upon the carved wooden screen and stalls of the choir, nestling among the scroll-work of the panels of the screen, and perched upon the stall-ends, each standard of which was surmounted by a seated figure in academic robes, carved with great dignity and skill."* (Morgan, 1914).

Clay (1861) also described this woodwork as being *"profusely adorned with the mitre, and cock and globe, the two badges of Bishop Alcock, the founder of the college. In one part we have representations of horse-shoes, pincers, nails, &c., all emblems of the trade of a smith, or rather a farrier, though the reasons for their introduction is unknown to us. Could it be, that some member of a family, like the Ferrars (ferrarius), who bore, at least, horse-shoes in their arms, was concerned in causing the wood-work to be originally executed?"*

Close examination of the woodwork in All Saints' Landbeach at the present time does not reveal any evidence of the Alcock crest (Fig. 37), so we may conclude that this distinctively marked 16th century woodwork brought from Jesus College chapel did not remain in the church after the restoration carried out by Walker in 1878. However, the 'farrier' pew front is still present (Fig. 38).

Fig. 37 Bishop Alcock's rebus (from Jesus College Chapel)

Fig. 38 Farrier's tools on pew front

Walker's notes indicate that after his reordering it was the pew front near the south door, and during the second half of the 20th century it was located on the north side set of western nave pews. In the 2006 re-ordering it was placed at the front of the north side nave pews.

In 1846 Jesus College once again refurnished its chapel and *"The College would have been glad to have recovered the old carved wood from Landbeach, but the Vicar and Churchwardens could not be brought to part with it. At a later date (1878), however, when Landbeach Church was under restoration, the architect rejected some fragments of the wood, which were bought by the College... The pulpit and part of the screen still remain at Landbeach. A handsome carved oak door, now in the south transept of the Cathedral at Ely, was also once, there can be little doubt, in Jesus Chapel. It was taken to Ely from Landbeach."* (Morgan, 1914).

Concerning the return of this woodwork, there is a letter in the archives of Jesus College, Cambridge (1846) from the Revd John Tinkler (Rector of Landbeach 1843 - 1871) to the Master & Fellows of Jesus College Cambridge dated 10 February 1846 that reads as follows:

"Gentlemen,

The Church Wardens of our Parish have given me the authority to state that they cannot, from a sense of duty, allow any thing to be removed from our Parish Church. I trust that the refusal of our Church Wardens to accede to your wishes will not materially interfere with so laudable an endeavour to restore & beautify your Chapel.

I am, Gentlemen
*Your humble serv*ᵗ
J. Tinkler"

Most of this woodwork did eventually go back to the College, although there was some dispute about the manner in which it was advertised for sale and the price to be paid! (Walker, 1879b). This woodwork was held by Landbeach Church *"from 1787 to 1879 (though much of it, including the ornamented stall ends and miserere . . was never fixed in position, but stored away in the vestry and elsewhere)"* (Walker, 1879a). Walker illustrated some of the Jesus College woodwork returned to the College, including the stall ends and tracery. The design of this tracery (Fig. 39) is very like that on the pulpit in Landbeach church (Fig. 40).

Walker (1879a) believed that *"The stalls, four in number, standing in the Landbeach chancel, obviously did not come from Jesus College. They seem to have formed, with the screen and pulpit, parts of a single composition."* Mr George Wood, one of the church architects, in his notes cited by Walker, commented that *"The original arrangement of the wood-work at the entrance to the chancel we found in situ; it was evidently made for the church, and not adapted, (and probably was coeval with the clerestory windows and the roof as readapted."*

"The pulpit was part of the original early screen and built out of it . . some of the panels from Jesus College were utilised and planted within the chamfers."

The chancel screen was standing in 1757, or a little earlier. Walker (1879a) noted that 'Cole has an entry that Mr Masters [Rector 1756 - 1797] about that date *"took the screen between the nave and chancel quite away, and removed the pulpit and desk to the south side of the chancel."'*

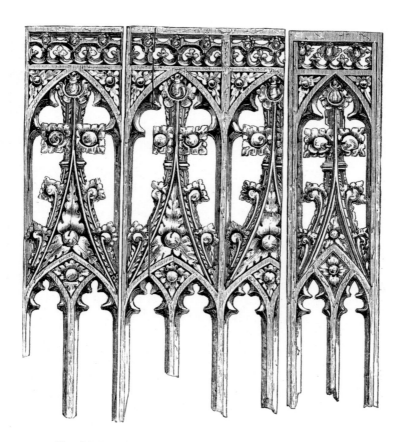

Fig. 39 Drawing of woodwork from Jesus College
(From Walker, 1879a)

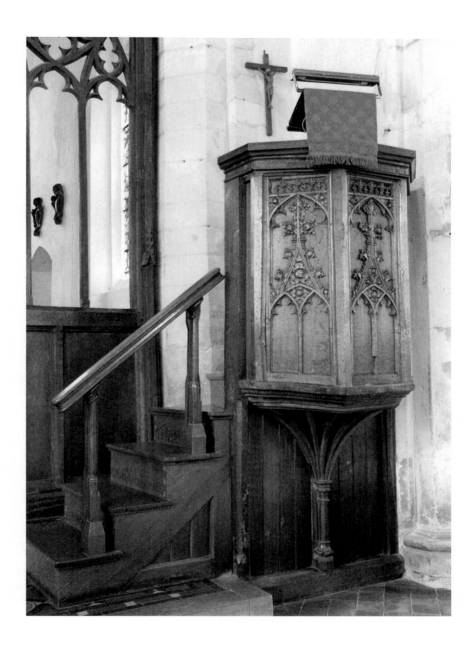

Fig. 40 Pulpit

NORTH DOOR

Masters (1756 - 1798) recorded that *"In 1787 R.M."* [i.e. Masters himself] *"gave to the church the picture of the Adoration of the Shepherds, said to be by a good hand and very valuable, with the beautiful carved door from Bp Alcock's chapel, wainscot and rails adjoining."*

Walker (1879a) noted that the door mentioned *"was in Landbeach Church in 1827, as G. R. Boissier describes it in his Notes on the Cambridgeshire Churches. It was given back to the Dean and Chapter of Ely subsequently by Mr Addison, Rector from 1821 to 1843, and is now placed at the entrance to the vestry in the south transept of the Cathedral."* (Fig. 41).

Bossier (1827) actually believed that *"The north door formerly belonged to Ely Cathedral: it is well carved in panels, some of which have relief in parts and fronts of cathedrals; mitres form a principal ornament; the door is very thick, the carvings very deep, and the whole well finished; but it is rather curious than valuable."*

Clay (1861) gave a fuller account of the loss of the north door. He described how the Revd Henry Fardell, on becoming the vicar of Waterbeach in 1821, persuaded the Landbeach rector, the Revd Edward Addison (without asking permission of the parish authorities) to allow him to appropriate this door. He gave it to the Dean and Chapter of Ely and replaced it with a plain oak one. The beautifully carved door was installed in the cathedral in 1840. Fardell seems to have acted on the notion that the door was intimately connected with and therefore ought to be preserved in the cathedral where Alcock, the founder of Jesus College, had been bishop.

Fig. 41 Door of the Canon's vestry, Ely Cathedral

It seems more likely, however, from Masters' own notes cited above that the location of Alcock's chapel is the one in Jesus College rather than Ely Cathedral.

In his description of the South East Transept of Ely Cathedral, the Clerk of Works John Bacon (1871) wrote that in 1840

"the Vergers' vestry was rearranged, an entrance was made from the Nave of the Transept thro the centre of the screen in the middle bay, and the very beautiful oak door inserted having its styles with the tops and three Munnions covered with running ornamental foliage, the Grapes and Leaf deeply cut; the bottom rail consists of four deep cut quatre foils with a Tudor rose in the centre; over each of these is a bracket and carved representations of a domed building under a rather flat canopy; in the middle rail is Bishop Alcock's favourite device, a cock standing on a Globe, repeated four times; but only one has the bird remaining; above are four brackets for the support of statues, over which were canopies and finished with tracery. This door was bought at an Auction Sale of old building materials at Landbeach - and afterwards repaired and presented by the late Canon Fardell, to the Cathedral and is now the door of the Canons' Vestry."

Mr Peter Meadows, Keeper of the Ely Dean and Chapter Archives, has commented (pers. comm.) that *"It is possible that Clay's account of Fardell's acquiring the door direct from the Rector is more accurate than Bacon's assertion that he bought it at auction; but there are no further records of the circumstances surrounding its installation in the Cathedral."*

Fig. 42 The Adoration of the Shepherds by Joachim Beuckeleur

ALTAR PICTURE

I n passing, we can note that the large picture, *The Adoration of the Shepherds* painted by Joachim Beuckeleur in 1562 (Fig. 42), had hung on the east wall behind the altar in Landbeach church from 1787, the gift of Robert Masters as recorded above. It no longer fitted below the east window when the floor of the chancel was raised in 1878. It was first removed to the Rectory, and before the Rectory was sold into private hands in 1977 the picture was put in store, first in Corpus Christi College, Cambridge, and subsequently the Fitzwilliam Museum, Cambridge until 1981. Then it was sold at auction at Sotheby's, raising £21,000 towards the restoration of the north aisle of the church carried out in 1983. This sale is recorded on a plaque by the north door of All Saints' (Fig. 43), together with a copy of the painting and a picture of the Revd Robert Masters. The latter is an engraving *"made by an artist named Facius from a drawing in 1796 by the Rev. Thomas Kerrich, a most intimate friend, Librarian to the University of Cambridge"* (Clay 1861).

Fig. 43 Plaques by north door

EAST WINDOW

The east window of All Saints' Church appears as a great jumble of images (Fig. 44). Ravensdale commented (1986) that *"These fragments have been fitted together into a frame that was never meant to take them. The quality of most of the glass, as well as the quantity, is very rare for a small parish church. Some of the fragments, especially those of very intense colour, are exceptionally old. The heads seem to be fifteenth century, and the one at the top, with his armillary sphere, could be one of the sea-travellers going to the new worlds. The lovely Madonna-like head in the centre is thought to be Lady Margaret Beaufort, with her parents, the grand-parents of Henry VII on either side."*

Ravensdale also comments that the armillary sphere was used for navigation in the late fourteenth and fifteenth centuries, and points out that there is a king struck in the eye by an arrow, comforting angels and horny devils, and running through all, men at prayer.

Some of the detailed figures mentioned are illustrated in Fig. 45.

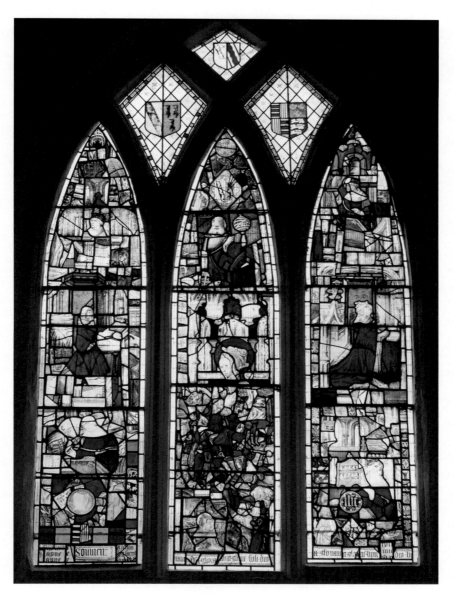

Fig. 44 East window

Lady Margaret Beaufort
Fig. 45a Details of figures in the East Window

Duke & Duchess of Somerset
Fig. 45b Details of figures in the East Window

Angel & Devil
Fig. 45c Details of figures in the East Window

Navigator
Fig. 45d Details of figures in the East Window

Arrow in the eye
Fig. 45e Details of figures in the East Window

Clay put forward the view (1861) that *"The East window, which was repaired, (in a very ordinary manner,) and glazed, by Mr Masters soon after his induction to the living, contains some good painted French glass of French manufacture transferred thither by him from the parlour window of the rectory house ... In the same window Mr Masters likewise put two heads, 'being thought by them, whose judgement may be relied on, worthy of preservation.' They are, he conceived, the heads of John Beaufort, and Margaret his wife, first duke and duchess of Somerset, parents of Margaret, countess of Richmond, so great a benefactress to the university of Cambridge; and they came from an oratory erected to the memory of her, her family and friends. Some heads of her friends, or relatives, have been added. The painted glass, being a compound of independent pieces, cannot of necessity present any regular subject."*

There is a strong tradition that the glass came from Wimborne Minster in Dorset, and was brought to Landbeach by Robert Masters while Rector of Landbeach. The Revd Jas. M. J. Fletcher, the Vicar of Wimborne Minster, wrote in his parish magazine (1908):

'Historical Note.
A little pamphlet, entitled Souvent me Souvient, has been sent to me by Rev. W. A. Cox, who is, I believe, a Fellow of St John's College, Cambridge (one of Lady Margaret's foundations). It contains an article, by Mr Cox, which is reprinted from the Eagle, St John's College Magazine (vol. xxvi., No. 137, June, 1905). The words mean "I often remember," or "I often bethink me," – and written in full would be Souvent il me Souvient. They occur in some modern stained glass at S. John's College, Cambridge, and in four different places at Christ's College, another of Lady Margaret's foundations, in the same university. Three of these are modern: but the fourth is in a portrait of Lady Margaret, on the west wall of the College Chapel, which portrait is supposed to be of the time of Queen Elizabeth. No doubt the modern inscriptions are taken from this. Mr Cox thinks that it was the family motto. I think it was more likely a motto adopted by herself, and, as will be seen below, showing her devotion to her courageous father, who died, it will be remembered,

when she was quite a child, - and to her mother; - or perhaps it marked her love for God and her knowledge of His purpose in her life. But it is not to the motto that I wish to draw your attention, but to what follows in the paper: At "Landbeach Church, some five miles from Cambridge, there are to be seen in the north and south lights of the east window, two figures which are believed to represent ... John, first Duke of Somerset and his Duchess. The window is composed of fragments, more or less considerable, of evidently ancient glass which were put together and placed in their present position by the eminent antiquarian, Robert Masters, who was Rector of Landbeach, 1759 - 1781 [sic]. Dr. Bryan Walker, formerly Law Lecturer in this College (S. John's) and Rector of Landbeach, 1871-1887, also a learned antiquary, who wrote a volume of Collectanea de Landbeche, still in manuscript, on the antiquities of his Church and parish, accepted this identification, which he gives in a notice of Landbeach contributed by him to Spalding's Guide to Cambridge. From Mrs. Bryan Walker, to whose kindness I am indebted for the above information, I further learn that on a visit to Wimborne many years ago, Dr Walker found a similar tradition there also as to the removal of a window containing the figures in question. The figure in the south light of the window now at Landbeach, is that of a lady of high rank kneeling, beneath a canopy, at a table on which is an open book of devotions. The face is towards the spectator's right, and the whole, save for the unlikeness of the face, strikingly resembles the familiar portraits of the Lady Margaret. The male figure is also canopied and kneeling at a desk with an open book, but the lower part is gone. Now beneath the figure of the lady, and clearly, I think, belonging to it, is the word souvient. The rest of the motto, it seems probable, originally stood beneath the male figure on the left. In that case it would appear that the words in question were the motto (or a motto) of the Beauforts."

'Does this tradition still exist? Have any of our readers ever heard that a window was removed from the Minster 150 years ago and placed elsewhere (eventually in Landbeach Church).'

Fletcher wrote again in his parish magazine (1911) about his holiday in the Eastern Counties:

"On the way from Ely to Cambridge I stopped at Landbeach to look at the East window in the Church which was spoken of in our Magazine some two or three years ago. It may be remembered that it was stated that there is a tradition that the window in question had originally been in Wimborne Minster, and that many years ago it was sold and placed in Landbeach Church. Although there is no ground for this tradition, the window unmistakably has to do with Lady Margaret Beaufort, the foundress of the Grammar School at Wimborne. She herself figures on the window, as do, probably, her parents, whose tomb is in our Minster."

We may reasonably deduce that since there is no mention of a response to the original question posed three years earlier as to the removal of the window from Wimborne to Landbeach that no one was able to supply such evidence.

Finally, we can note that Jones & Underwood (1992) accepted the Wimborne Minster connection with Landbeach when they wrote:

"The tour of 1496 allowed the royal entourage to halt at Wimborne Minster, resting place of Margaret's parents. Here is a memorial window to John Beaufort Duke of Somerset and his wife Margaret (the remains of the glass were later transferred to the parish church of Landbeach, Cambridgeshire), and a fine alabaster tomb."

Clay (1861) records that *"In the upper tracery of this window are three coats of arms. One of them is too indistinct to be made out: another has quarterly 1, 4, argent, 3 bars, gules; 2, 3, paly of six, or, and gules, impaling France and England per fesse[3]; the third, (which has been reversed by the glazier,) argent, on a bend engrailed, sable, 3 fishes,*

---

3 *"It has been suggested, that these were the arms of the De Beche family"* [who held the original manor house to the east of the church and presented the first rector whose name we know, to the living (Clay, 1861)].

argent, impaling, or, three lions rampant, sable."

Walker (1871-1887) records that *"The coats of arms in the upper compartments of the East window were replaced by more perfect copies, painted by Mrs Walker in 1880; and the originals after repair were placed in other windows of the church."* The coats of arms are illustrated in Fig. 46. They are made up of a number of different features, including arms reminiscent of Chamberlayne, dolphins, dragon's heads, and parts of the Royal Arms of England from the accession of Henry IV until the end of the reign of Elizabeth I. Their significance is not known.

Fig. 46 Coats of arms in the upper tracery of the East Window

The East window had to be repaired after the end of the 1939-45 war, for it had been damaged by an explosion on the neighbouring airfield at Waterbeach. It took some time to get the necessary materials as the whole window needed re-leading, but the window had been repaired and replaced by October 1947 (Landbeach PCC, 1937 - 1959).

THE VICTORIAN RESTORATION

The appearance of the church as Walker found it can be seen in photographs (Fig. 47) taken before his restoration work (Corpus Christi College, Cambridge, 1878) as well as the architects' plans (Cambridgeshire Archives, 1878a). Before 1878 there were box pews, particularly in the north and south aisles; a vestry in the northwest corner; the font near the north door; a lumber and store area to the left inside the south door; and a harmonium in front of the tower (Fig. 48). A coke stove (with no chimney!) occupied the middle of the nave aisle; and the pulpit, in its present position on the south side, had a sounding board over the top. There was no screen across the chancel arch, and the east end of the north aisle and the north arch of the chancel were walled-up.

In 1878 Walker endeavoured to restore the church to what he considered to be its original arrangement. He unblocked the arches from the north aisle and the chancel into the former Lady Chapel, and uncovered three piscenas or niches with perforated basins for washing the vessels used at Holy Communion. There is a square double Early English one in the sanctuary (Fig. 49); an Early English piscina and credence (the shelf for holding the Communion elements before consecration) in a double arch at the east end of the south aisle (Fig. 50) – the presumed St James' Chapel of the early church (see Fig. 10); and a Decorated piscina in what is now the vestry and was formerly the Lady Chapel (Fig. 51). Such features usually are found on the south side of an altar.

Fig. 47 Photographs of the church before the 1878 restoration –
courtesy of the Master and Fellows of Corpus Christi College, Cambridge
(Corpus Christi College, Cambridge, 1878)

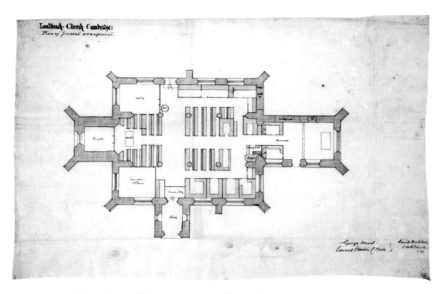

*Fig. 48 Architects' plan before the 1878 restoration
(Cambridgeshire Archives, 1878a)*

It can be seen from the photograph taken prior to the restoration in 1878 (Corpus Christi College, Cambridge, 1878) that the stalls in the chancel originally faced east (Fig. 47 upper). Walker turned the seats so as to face north and south in collegiate style and thus leave a passage of reasonable width to the Holy Table.

It is not clear why the final result of Walker's work was not completely in agreement with the plans, and a drawing (Fig. 52) made by the architect, E. Francis Clarke, of the proposed appearance (Cambridgeshire Archives, 1878b, c). In particular, a chancel screen was introduced by moving the screen then in the tower arch, and the chancel roof was not rebuilt.

Clay (1861) records that *"the present rector* [the Revd John Tinkler, who immediately preceded Bryan Walker] *... laid out, soon after his induction* [in 1843], *large sums of money upon the rectory-house, and the chancel of the church, which are both now in good condition."*

Fig. 49 Piscina in the
Sanctuary

Fig. 50 Piscina in the South Aisle

Fig. 51 Piscina in the vestry

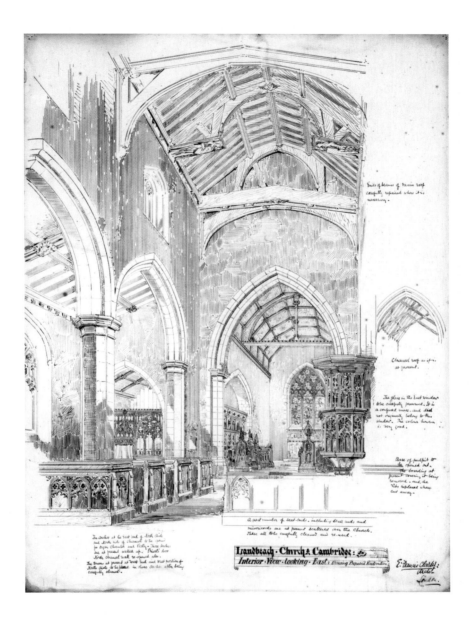

*Fig. 52 Architects' drawing of proposed restoration in 1878
(Cambridgeshire Archives, 1878 c)*

Clay identifies (1861) in fact that *"He [Tinkler] put on an entirely new roof"* which may be why it was not remodelled by Walker.

The font moved by Walker from near the north door to a position centrally in front of the tower (Fig. 53) comprised a marble basin placed by Masters on the old stem, itself replaced in 1846 (Victoria County History, 1989b).

Walker did provide a new communion table and altar rails (Fig. 54). He wrote (1871 - 1887) that *"The carved woodwork inserted in the front of the Communion Table was in 1878 found, covered thickly with paint, at the top of the wainscoting of the chancel pew on the N. side. The carving in the legs of the table came from the top of the doorway in the W. screen, which in 1878 was removed to the E. This Communion Table was made by Mr Clipsham in 1878; the old Communion Table, a very small and mean one, is now part of the furniture of the vestry; so also is a still older one with a drawer."*

"The altar-rails were given in 1884 by Mr W. Cory Daniell, and were made by Jonathan Haird of Landbeach at the price of £7.15/-."

We may note that both the old communion tables (Fig. 55) are probably Jacobean (Ravensdale, 1986); the latter is still in the vestry, while the former has been used in various parts of the church, including as a nave altar.

Fig.53 Font

Fig. 54 Communion table

Fig. 55 Jacobean tables

When Walker removed the wainscot boarding of the pulpit the remains of wall painting were exposed (Fig. 56). The motif of a red vine scroll decorated with grapes has been dated to the early part of the 14th century on stylistic grounds (Tobit Curteis *pers comm.*). Much more of the church had been similarly decorated (Keyser, 1883). This was *"apparently the pattern used to fill up the spaces between the numerous pictures of saints and groups of figures with which we know the walls to have been covered. Several of these were in existence till 1857, when the old colour wash was removed preparatory to recolouring."* (Walker, 1879a).

The frescoes were entirely destroyed when the authorities of the day chipped the walls in order to secure a new coating of plaster (Walker, 1879a), although there are still faint traces of colour on the arch at the east end of the north aisle. However, close examination of the photograph of the east end of the church prior to 1878 (Fig. 47 lower) reveals a text above and following the curve of the east window arch:

"And The Word Became Flesh."

Fig. 56 Vine scroll wall decoration by pulpit

Fig. 57a. Nave looking west, 1900

Fig. 57b Nave looking east, 1900

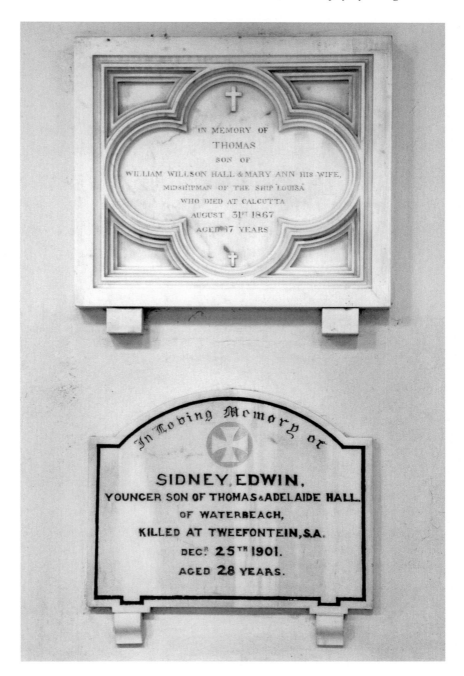

Fig. 58 Plaques on north wall

Walker collected the few old open pews that were in the western part of the centre aisle and placed these together in the south aisle. Confirmation of the date of photographs (Fig. 57a, b) designated as taken about 1900 (Cambridgeshire Archives, 1900) is given by the fact that a plaque put up on the north wall in 1902 (Fig. 58) is not evident in the picture in which the plaque above it dating from 1867 is visible (Fig. 57b). The older plaque is just visible on the east wall of the north aisle in the photograph taken before the 1878 restoration (Fig. 47 lower). The plaque obviously had to be moved when Walker unblocked the arch leading to what became the organ chamber. The views looking both east and west in the church show that there were no fixed pews at the western end of the nave. The benches visible are the moveable ones now housed in the 16th century Tithe Barn that stands to the south east of the church. A parishioner of long-standing (and organist for more than 50 years) Miss Jean Turner recalled that these benches were in place in the 1930s, when a member of the congregation with a wooden leg found it easier to sit there rather than in the fixed pews.

A plaque in the south porch records the free availability of the seating in the church from the Victorian restoration (Fig. 59).

The three front pews in the south aisle were removed in 1952 when the Chapel dedicated to St James was refurbished in memory of the Revd Ronald K. Denham, Rector 1922 – 1948 (Fig. 60). The Bishop of Ely consecrated the restored Chapel on 11 January 1953 and the Citation for this work (Cambridgeshire Archives, 1951) stated *"That the work will involve the removal of three 16th century oak pews which will be placed at the back of the Nave where there are four pitch pine pews (one damaged) which will be scrapped."*

Fig. 59 South Porch plaque

Fig. 60 Denham plaque in south aisle

Examination of the pews at the western end of the nave (Fig. 61) confirmed that the pew front and rear seat on the south side matched the pews in the south aisle. The short pew between them against the pillar was modern. On the north side, the two rear pews again matched those in the south aisle, but with a modern seat in one, and a short modern pew against the pillar.

All these western pews were moved in 2006 and placed against the walls and elsewhere in the church. This created an open area around the font when the decayed wooden floors in the nave and aisles were replaced and a new heating system installed.

Fig.61 Nave west end prior to re-ordering in 2006

ANGEL LECTERN

A particularly striking item of the furnishings in All Saints' Church, and one that attracts considerable attention, is the wooden lectern in the form of an angel (Fig. 62). Walker's notes (1871-87) state that *"The lectern, an angel carved in oak with extended wings, was bought of Mr Greenwood, dealer in antiquities, Stone Gate, York, in 1882, for the price of £13.10/-, which money was raised by subscription of the parishioners. It came from a church in Holland, but Mr Greenwood could give no further particulars, except that it formed part of a large composition used as a pulpit, and having in the centre a figure of St Michael trampling on the dragon, placed in front of a panel; two side panels with the angel and another of similar kind, with uplifted hands supporting a projecting upper tier of panels. Containing smaller figures and surmounted [by] a carved canopy, above which came the preacher's desk."*

This information presumably formed the basis of the comments by Nikolaus Pevsner (2002) who described the lectern as *"Large, very splendid, utterly un-English. Seated angel, holding the book-rest. It is said to have been the support of a Dutch pulpit (bought from an antique dealer in York in 1882). That may well be true; the date would then be the early or mid C17."*

The date given means that the lectern arrived in All Saints' a little after Walker carried out his restoration work on the church, but strangely the angel is not visible in the photographs taken in the church about 1900 (Figs 57a, b).

Fig. 62 Angel lectern

MEMORIALS

A t the west end of the church on either side of the tower arch are two fine marble tomb slabs. The black one on the south side (Fig. 63) commemorates William Rawley, Rector of Landbeach 1617 – 1667. He was Sir Francis Bacon's Secretary and later Chaplain to both Charles I and his son Charles II. A shield at the head has Rawley's arms to the right of those of Wickstead, which is not the usual arrangement and so perhaps the engraver's mistake. When he moved to Landbeach Rawley married Barbara, the daughter of John Wickstead, an Alderman and Mayor of Cambridge, and Principal of Bernards Inn London. John Wickstead was buried in Landbeach on 5 January 1646 aged 83 years (Cambridgeshire Archives, 2004). Rawley, as proctor of the clergy of the diocese of Ely, subscribed his assent to the newly revised Book of Common Prayer on 20 December 1661.

Clay (1861) commented that *"His son William, . . his wife, and all his servants, were carried off by the plague in 1666, which calamity so greatly affected him, that he died the following year, and was buried, 20ᵗʰ June, in the chancel of his church. He, and Henry Clifford, had held the living 97 years between them. Upon William Rawley's death the college presented Francis Wilford, D.D. master, and dean of Ely, 22ⁿᵈ June 1667, who died the 18ᵗʰ of the next month, and could hardly, therefore, have done anything towards taking possession."*

Fig. 63 Tomb slab of William Rawley

Fig. 64 Tomb slab of John Cory

In the nave floor on the north side of the tower arch there is the slab of John Cory (Fig.64), Rector 1683 - 1727, sadly now water stained. Masters (1756 - 98) notes that in the chancel *"under a black Marble Slab are deposited the Remains of Dr Rawley within the Rails & those of Mr John Cory, a large Freestone without (but removed upon new paving the Chancel) with inscriptions."*

This must mean that they were placed elsewhere in the chancel, for Walker (1871 - 87) wrote that *"Cory's and Rawley's tombstones were removed in 1878 to the west end of the church; the consent of the Cory family being first obtained. This was done because their retention in situ would have prevented our restoring the original levels of the chancel floor, of which we had abundant indications when we took up the pavement."*

Walker's note continues (1871 - 87)

"The tombstones of Thomas Cooke Burroughes and his son, and that of Mr Addison were placed beneath the chancel tiling (also by consent of their representatives) and marble tablets inserted as nearly as possible where the tombstones lay originally.

The Misses Sproules were not buried in the chancel, but the brass-plate in the chancel floor was placed there by their sister, Miss Sproule of Bath, instead of a small freestone slab there previously and having on it merely their initials and the dates of their death."

This brass plate (Fig. 65) actually says that the remains of the two sisters, granddaughters of Robert Masters, are buried beneath, and the church burial register records the funerals of both sisters in 1813.

Marble tablets in the chancel floor record the burial of the both the Burroughes men (Fig. 66), and also Edward Addison (Fig. 67). The large tomb slab inscribed with the names of Thomas Cooke Burroughes and his son Robert Masters Burroughes still lies in the void under the wooden flooring of the choir stalls on the south side of the chancel (Fig. 68). A smaller stone engraved in three lines with the initials '*E. A.*', '*M. S. A.*' and the date '*1843*' is in the bottom of the void under the flooring of the choir stalls on the north side (Fig. 69). A plaque to Edward Addison (Rector 1821 - 1843) and his sister Maria Sarah, who died barely two months before him in 1843, is on the north wall of the chancel to the west of the organ (Fig. 70). Below is a brass plaque commemorating the Revd John Tinkler, who succeeded him as Rector, 1843 – 71.

Fig. 65 Brass plate in Chancel floor for the Misses Sproules

Fig. 66 Floor tablet for Burroughes burials

Fig. 67 Floor tablet for Addison

Fig. 68 Burroughes tomb slab under south choir stalls floor

Fig. 69 Addison tomb slab under north choir stall floor

Fig. 70 Addison memorial plaque

Fig. 71 Monuments to John Micklebourgh & his wife

Fig. 72 Clifford plaque

At the eastern end of the chancel north wall there are two large tablets (Fig. 71) in memory of John Micklebourgh (Rector 1727 – 1756 and Professor of Chemistry in the University of Cambridge) and his wife. Masters (1756 - 98) described these as *"two handsome Marble Monuments for Mr <u>Micklebourgh</u> & his Wife, with <u>Taylor's</u> (name as an insert, replacing 'a') Coat of Arms on a Shield between them, whose Remains were deposited in a Vault underneath. There is likewise between them a small Brass Plate within a Stone Frame in memory of <u>Henry Clifford</u>."*

Clay (1861) notes that *"The name of Taylor, or Tayler, ... has been common in the parish for a very long period, and still exists there. William Taylor was one of the churchwardens for 1540, and the two succeeding years. The first of the family, who, having bought property at Landbeach, settled on it, was, most likely, a son of Sir William Taylor, Knt., lord mayor of London in 1469. He could hardly have been the lord mayor himself."*

Ravensdale (1986) quotes the inventory and furnishings of the Taylor house in 1691, now known as Old Beach Farm, showing the substantial means of the family.

The Landbeach Parish Registers (Cambridgeshire Archives, 2004) list members of the Taylor family as Churchwardens at Landbeach in 1660 and 1661 (Robert), 1663, 1664, 1666 (William), 1683, 1685 (John), 1685 (William), 1729 (James and Rivers), 1755 (William), 1756 (William jun), 1756, 1760 (Uriah), 1763, 1765, 1769, 1775 (William), The coat of arms presumably refers to one of these men. At the time of the inclosure, 1806, the Taylors were the largest resident landowners in Landbeach (Victoria County History, 1989a).

The plaque to Henry Clifford (Rector 1570 - 1617) is set into the north wall of the chancel (Fig. 72) above the doorway to the vestry and between the Micklebourgh memorials. Henry Clifford's son John travelled to Holland and became a deacon of the English

Congregation of Reformed Christians in Amsterdam. A stained glass window featuring the Clifford arms appears in the New Church, Amsterdam (Brian Macdonald-Milne *pers. comm.*) There is a strong Clifford Society with an international membership that visit Landbeach occasionally.

One tombstone of unknown origin in the church is a large carved coffin lid (Fig. 73). It was more or less in front of the north door in 1861 when Clay (1861) described it as *"The beautifully raised cross slab in the pavement, partly of the north aisle, partly of the vestry"* (which was then in the north west corner). He referred to an engraving by Cutts (1849) who assigned it to the 13th century and thus a relic of an earlier church. Gough (1796) also included this stone in his illustrations. The carving has deteriorated considerably since these drawings were made (Fig. 74). The slab was moved in the 1878 restoration when the Victorian tiles were laid down to replace the original stone flooring. Walker's notes record that

"there was a handsome slab of 13th century work, or rather one that had been handsome, placed exactly across the entrance to the N. door. This from its position had been much worn down by passing footsteps and a deep groove had been cut across the middle in order to fasten firmly the screen which partitioned off the vestry from the nave so that although the attempt to remove it was made carefully the stone broke into several fragments."

The slab was moved again in the re-ordering carried out in 2006, and is now fixed vertically to the north wall of the nave arcade at the west end to prevent further wear.

Fig. 73 Medieval coffin lid

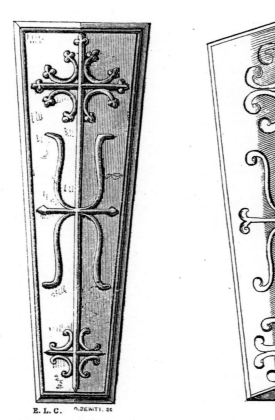

E. L. C.   ∩.JEWITT. sc
LANDBEACH. CAMBRIDGESHIRE.

Fig. 74 Engravings from Gough 1796 & Cutts 1849
of medieval coffin lid

The photograph of the Communion Table (Fig. 54) shows two fine brass candle sticks. These were a gift from Mrs Ellen Hatfield, in memory of her parents William and Edith Money, dedicated at Easter 1913. Mr Money had been a pillar of the church and Churchwarden for many years.

The most recent memorial (Fig. 75) records that Matthew Parker was Rector of Landbeach 1545 - 1554 while Master of Corpus Christi College. It is a handsome plaque above the squint at the east end of the north aisle arcade and was commissioned by the College and installed at the suggestion of a parishioner and Life Fellow of Robinson College, Cambridge, the Revd Dr Peter Newman Brooks. The plaque was made by Mark Bury of Oakington, the son of a Fellow and Librarian of Corpus Christi College, Dr Patrick Bury and dedicated in 1987 (Brian Macdonald–Milne *pers. comm.*).

Parker wrote in his Journal for 2nd April 1554 that he was *"Deprived of my Rectory of Landbeach"* on the accession of Queen Mary for being married and on the side of the reformers (Denham, 1925c). He retired with his family to Norfolk, but was subsequently appointed Archbishop of Canterbury under Queen Elizabeth I. Matthew Parker created one of the finest libraries of medieval manuscripts in the country when authorised by the Privy Council in 1568 to collect ancient books and manuscripts that might otherwise be lost through the dispersal of the monastic libraries. On his death in 1575 these books and documents were left to Corpus Christi College with strict instructions on their care and now reside in its Parker Library.

Fig. 75 Matthew Parker plaque

Fig. 75 Matthew Parker plaque

Fig. 76 Plaques to recent parishioners

There are three pottery memorials to 20th century parishioners, on the west walls of the north and south aisles and in the chancel between the screen and organ (Fig. 76). These were all executed by Derek Andrews of the former Prickwillow Pottery.

OTHER STAINED GLASS

Mrs Fanny Walker was a skilled artist. She painted the glass for the window illustrating the Ascension in the south wall of the chancel above the Rector's stall (Fig. 77), given as a thank offering in 1880 for the restoration of the church. This window includes a coat of arms on the lower border incorporating her husband's arms and her own (Fig. 78):

Blazon: argent a chevron sable between three Cornish choughs proper (Walker) impaling gules a lion rampant reguardant argent between three wells masoned (Wells).

[a black chevron on a silver background between three Cornish choughs on the left; an erect silver lion between three brick wells on a red background to the right]

Mrs Walker's maiden name was Wells, as shown by the Banns of Marriage read in All Saints' Church on 31 March 1872 by her husband-to-be, and she came from Airmyn in Yorkshire (Cambridgeshire Archives, 2004).

Fig. 77 Ascension window

Fig. 78 Walker & Wells arms in the Ascension window

Mrs Walker also painted the east window in the south aisle (Fig. 79) from designs prepared by Mr W H Constable of Cambridge. This depicts Christ's Sermon on the Mount, and was placed there in memory of her husband by his sorrowing widow whom she survived for 40 years.

Bryan Walker's likeness is represented in the purple-robed figure on the left of the window (see Walker, 1871-1887). The face of this figure, shown in profile (Fig. 80), is indeed remarkably similar to a photograph of Bryan Walker (Fig. 81) removed from the Rectory on its sale in 1975.

 It may well have formed the model for the window image.

Fig. 79 Walker memorial window depicting the Sermon on the Mount

Fig. 80 The Revd Bryan Walker, in south aisle window

Fig. 81 Photo of the Revd Bryan Walker

Walker (1879) reconstructed the stonework of the window at the east end of the south aisle, because the arch that had led into the Chamberlayne mortuary chapel was in a ruinous state, built without proper foundations across what had previously been the interior of the church. There are two defaced figures on either side of the window, presumably surviving from the earlier archway. Clay (1861) describes the one on the north side *"on a stone shield, which a mutilated angel is holding upon his breast, and which may have once formed a bracket for an image, the arms of the see of Ely"* (Fig. 82).

Fig. 82 Mutilated Ely angel

An article in the Cambridge Chronicle dated 20 September 1879 records the following:

"LANDBEACH – *The Chancel of this parish church has this week been embellished by the insertion of a stained glass window in memory of the Rev. John Cory, B.D., rector from 1688 to 1727, and the Rev. Robert Masters, B.D., rector from 1756 to 1797. The funds for the window were raised by subscription among the descendants of the above named rectors, the Rev. E.W. Cory, vicar of Meldreth, having initiated the idea and by his diligent canvassing brought to a successful issue. The arms of Mr Cory occupy the head of the window, those of Mr Masters are placed in one of the side lights, and in the other the arms of Cory and Masters impalled, denoting that Mr Masters married Mr Cory's granddaughter. The window is the workmanship of Mr Ion Pace, 78, High Street, Camden Town, London, who deserves great praise for the excellence of his colours and design.*"

The arms in this window are illustrated in Fig. 83. John Cory was also vicar of Impington, and his eldest son, also named John, became vicar of Waterbeach in 1721 and succeeded his father at Impington on his death. In his will, John Cory senior left to his *"Well beloved son, John Cory Clerk, the coat of arms which for a long time hath gone with the family."* (Bedford-Groom, 2005). The Cory Society, with a world-wide membership, publishes the results of research into the family history.

Robert Masters was also vicar of Waterbeach from 1759 to 1784, succeeded by his son William. He retired from Landbeach to live in the Rectory with his son-in-law, Thomas Cooke Burroughes, who had succeeded his son as vicar of Waterbeach. Fellows of Colleges were not allowed to marry, until 1882, hence they often became incumbents of a parish near Cambridge to have a family.

Cory arms

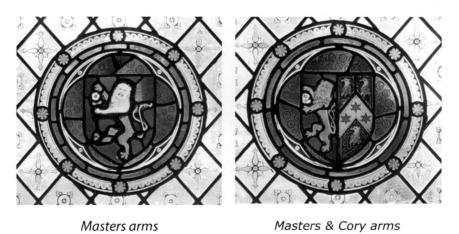

Masters arms   *Masters & Cory arms*

Fig. 83 Arms of Cory & Masters in the Sanctuary window

Clay (1861) thought *"All the windows of the church were at first filled with painted glass, of which no more remains, than what we see in the uppermost portions of some of them."* These medieval fragments in the windows of the south aisle are illustrated in Fig. 84.

Fig. 84 Medieval glass in the south aisle windows

Fig. 84 (Contd...) Medieval glass in the south aisle windows

ORGAN

The present organ (Fig. 85) was built and installed by J.W. Walker & Sons in 1906 (Dictionary of Organs and Organists, 1921). It has been maintained by the same firm ever since. It was said to have cost £350 (Kelly, 1916). The instrument has tracker action and full compass on both manuals and pedals. There are 4 stops on the great, 3 on the swell, 1 on the pedals and 4 couplers. The organ is now blown electrically but still retains the hand-operated bellows and has extending candlesticks on the console.

The Minutes of the Landbeach PCC meeting held on 20 January 1948 record:

"The Rector [the Revd R.K. Denham] *made reference to the sudden death of the organ blower Mr W. White. This meant a new organ blower was needed, and after a long discussion it was proposed by Mr W. Camps and Sec. by Miss Harrison that the salary be increased to £8-0-0 per year (with holidays). It was also proposed that we negotiate for an electric blower, and the Rector said that he would write to Messrs Walker (the builders) for prices etc."* Landbeach PCC, 1937 - 1959).

The following month a letter was read confirming the ordering of the electric blower for the organ, and at the May meeting a Resolution for a Faculty for the installation of the blower was passed. In July it was reported that Mr Leyland had been asked to put in an estimate for wiring and fixing the blower, and the Faculty was received in December 1948 (Landbeach PCC, 1937 - 1959)

Fig. 85 The organ

It was noted earlier that the architects' plan of the church before the 1878 restoration (p. 81, Fig. 48) marks a harmonium in front of the tower. Such an instrument is not immediately evident in this position in the photograph of the interior looking west taken before the 1878 restoration (Fig. 47), although it may be on the north side. There is a record (Langwill & Boston, 1970) that there was an anonymous barrel-organ in Landbeach church which was removed and after 23 years in a shed at Cottenham restored and brought to the Cambridge Folk Museum to illustrate a lecture by Canon Galpin in 1931. In 1938 it was stored in a derelict attic and in 1961 had become so damaged as to be beyond repair and was destroyed.

These dates suggest that the barrel-organ was removed from the church about 1908, that is, soon after the new Walker organ was installed.

BIER

In 1929 the Landbeach Women's Institute raised the funds to provide a wheeled bier for the use of the village (Denham, 1929). The bier is still kept in the church (Fig. 86), and although it was a great help at the time, it is not used now on a regular basis.

Fig. 86 Bier

CHURCHYARD

A ll Saints' Church is surrounded by a churchyard containing many burials, only some of which are marked with headstones. Clay (1861) said that at the time he wrote it contained two perches less than half an acre. New ground was added in 1872, and again in 1924 when the Revd R. K. Denham *"obtained permission from Corpus Christi College to give a rood of the Rectory paddock ... as an enlargement"* (1924a). The Bishop of Ely consecrated the new ground on 27 March 1927 (Denham, 1926).

The extent to which the old churchyard had been filled was revealed when foundations for the new North Porch were excavated outside the north door in 2006. The archaeologists found burials up to at least six graves deep between 0.55m and 1.40m+ below the present ground level, likely to date to the 18th and 19th centuries. A few medieval pottery sherds were also found, from the 12th to 14th centuries (Atkins, 2007). The density of burials and the village population numbers tally to suggest that there are likely to have been some 6,000 burials over the past 900 years in the churchyard. A plaque in the floor of the North Porch (Fig. 87) indicates where the disturbed burials were re-interred close to their original position.

The Cambridgeshire Family History Society has surveyed and recorded some two hundred of the inscriptions on the Landbeach churchyard monuments (Cambridgeshire Archives, 1985). From these data the oldest decipherable headstones appear to be a series stretching away to the south from the priest's door (Fig. 88). They relate to the Taylor family, noted

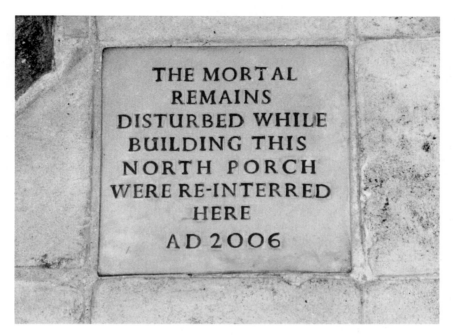

Fig. 87 Floor plaque

Fig. 88 Oldest headstones

above as the largest resident landowners in the village during the 18th century. They include Robert Taylor, the son of William and Joane who died 3 May 1691 aged 66; Alice Taylor, their daughter who died 19 August 1690 aged 46; William, another son, died 25 April 1684; and another daughter, Ann, who died 5 June 1692 aged 51.

The Revd Robert Masters was buried below the east window (Fig. 89). Members of his family, including his wife and son, and later Rectors are buried nearby.

In the south west angle of the tower and south aisle stands the village war memorial (Fig. 90). This is engraved with the names of the sixteen local men who died in the Great War 1914 - 1919, and two in the Second World War, 1939 - 1945. There is also a wooden war memorial inside the church (Fig. 91), at the east end of the north aisle, with the names of all the men who went from the village to serve in the First World War, and crosses beside those who did not return. There is some confusion over the names of the two H. J. Hattons, who were the cousins Herbert John and Harry. Only one name appears on the inside memorial, presumably because it was thought there was a mistaken duplication.

Fig. 89 Robert Masters' headstone

Fig. 90 War Memorial

Fig. 91 War Memorial in north aisle

CODA

A ll Saints' Church Landbeach today bears witness to its long history through the building itself, its stones, fabric and furnishings, as well as the written records preserved over the centuries. At the beginning of the 21st century since the birth of Jesus Christ it is still a focus of Christian worship and community activity for the village it serves. Now we have floodlighting, central heating and toilet facilities, features undreamed of by our forebears. And on the list of Rectors known since 1160 AD we have added the name of our first woman Priest, in charge of both this parish and our sister church, St John the Evangelist, in Waterbeach.

Times may change, together with the fashions of style, and the language of worship. But the church continues, to remind us of our rich heritage, our continuity with the past, and our hopes for the future under God.

REFERENCES

Anon. 1947. Hampton Court Bells. The Ringing World, September 19th, 1947.

Atkins, R. 2007. Late Post-Medieval Burials at All Saints Church, Landbeach, Cambridgeshire. Cambridgeshire County Council CAM ARC Report No. 859.

Bacon, J. 1871. A Record of the Restorations, Repairs etc done in and about Ely Cathedral since 1818. University Library, Cambridge: Ely Dean and Chapter Archives. EDC 4/6/2.

Bedford-Groom, D. 2005. An Afternoon of Discovery. Cory Society Newsletter No. 38, December 2005.

Bingley, F.J. & Cockerill, T.J. 2006. Cambridgeshire Church Heraldry. Cambridge.

Bossier, G.R. 1827. Notes on the Cambridgeshire Churches. London.

Cambridgeshire County Council, 1985. Historic Building Record, Landbeach.

Clay, W.K. 1861. A History of the Parish of Landbeach in the County of Cambridge, Deighton, Bell & Co., Cambridge.

Corpus Christi College, Cambridge, 1878. Landbeach Church before the restoration of 1878 (2 photographs). Archives of Corpus Christi College, Cambridge.

Cambridgeshire Archives [1878a]. Landbeach Church Cambridge: showing present arrangements (Architects drawing). P104/6/3.

Cambridgeshire Archives [1878b]. Landbeach Church Cambridge: proposed arrangements (Architects drawing). P104/6/3.

Cambridgeshire Archives [1878c]. Pen and ink drawing showing proposed plans for interior restoration of Landbeach Church by E. Francis Clarke. P103/104.

Cambridgeshire Archives [1900]. Landbeach Church. (2 photographs) P104/28/9 +10.

Cambridgeshire Archives [1951]. Citation for the Restoration of the South Aisle Chapel, 18 October 1951. P104/6/16.

Cambridgeshire Archives 1985. Monumental Inscriptions. All Saints' Church, Landbeach. Cambridgeshire Family History Society.

Cambridgeshire Archives 2004. Landbeach Register Transcript.

Cox, W.A., 1905. Souvent me Souvient. Eagle, XXVI, pp. 359 - 363.

Cutts, E.L. 1849. A Manual for the Study of the Sepulchral Slabs and Crosses of the Middle Ages, London.

Denham, R.K. 1923. All Saints', Landbeach, Monthly Magazine. Vol. 12 No. 11, November 1923.

Denham, R.K. 1924a. All Saints', Landbeach, Monthly Magazine. Vol. 13 No. 9, September 1924.

Denham, R.K. 1924b. . Notes on our History – VIII. All Saints', Landbeach, Monthly Magazine. Vol. 13 No. 11, November 1924.

Denham, R.K. 1925a. Notes on our History – X. All Saints', Landbeach, Monthly Magazine. Vol. 14 No. 1, January 1925.

Denham, R.K. 1925b. Notes on our History –XI. All Saints', Landbeach, Monthly Magazine. Vol. 14 No.2, February 1925.

Denham, R.K. 1925c. Notes on our History – XIV All Saints', Landbeach, Monthly Magazine. Vol. 14 No. 6, June 1925.

Denham, R.K. 1926. All Saints', Landbeach, Monthly Magazine. Vol. 15 No. 5, May 1926.

Denham, R.K. 1928. All Saints', Landbeach, Monthly Magazine. Vol. 17 No. 4, March 1928.

Denham, R.K. 1929. All Saints', Landbeach, Monthly Magazine. Vol. 18 No. 5, April 1929.

Denham, R.K. 1936. Landbeach Parish Magazine. October, 1936.

Dictionary of Organs and Organists, 1921. 2nd edition. Geo. Aug. Mate & Son, London.

Domesday Book. 2002. Alecto Historical Editions, Penguin Books.

Fairweather, J. 2005. Liber Eliensis. (English Translation). The Boydell Press, Woodbridge.

Fletcher, J.M.J. 1908. The Wimborne Minster Parish Magazine, September 1908.

Gambell, R. 2005. All Saints' Church Landbeach Explored. Mission Computers, Bourne, Cambridge.

Gough, R. 1796. Sepulchral Monuments in Great Britain applied to Illustrate the History of Families. Manners, Habits, and Arts. London.

Gray, R. & Stubbings, D. 2000. Cambridge Street Names. Their Origins and Associations. Cambridge University Press.

Jesus College, Cambridge, 1791. Accounts of Expense in fitting up the Chapel.1789-93. Chapel Box 1.

Jesus College, Cambridge, 1846. Letter from J.Tinkler. Chapel Box 2. 1845-80.

Jones, M.K. & Underwood, M.G. 1992. The King's Mother. Cambridge University Press.

Kelly's Directory of the Counties of Cambridgeshire, Norfolk and Suffolk, 1916.

Keyser, C.E. 1883. A List of Buildings Having Mural Decorations. 3rd ed. London.

Landbeach Parochial Church Council, 1937 - 1959. Minutes.

Langwill, L.G. & Boston, N. 1970. Church and Chamber Barrel-Organs. 2nd ed. Lyndesay G. Langwill, Edinburgh.

Masters, R. 1753. The History of Corpus Christi College Cambridge. Cambridge.

Masters, R., Rector of Landbeach 1756 - 98. Collectanea de Landbeach.Vol.1. Archives of Corpus Christi College, Cambridge.

Morgan, I & R. 1914. The Stones and Story of Jesus Chapel, Traced and Told by Iris & Gerda Morgan, Bowes & Bowes, Cambridge.

Pevsner, N. 2002. The Buildings of England: Cambridgeshire. Yale University Press, New Haven & London.

Ravensdale, J.R. 1974. Liable to Flood. Cambridge University Press.

Ravensdale, J.R. 1986. The Domesday Inheritance. Souvenir Press Ltd, London.

Rawle, T. 2005. Cambridge. Frances Lincoln Ltd, London.'

Victoria County History, 1989a. A History of the County of Cambridgeshire and the Isle of Ely. Vol.9. Chesterton, Northstowe, and Papworth Hundreds. Landbeach: Economic History. Oxford University Press.

Victoria County History, 1989b. A History of the County of Cambridgeshire and the Isle of Ely. Vol.9. Chesterton, Northstowe, and Papworth Hundreds. Landbeach Church. Oxford University Press.

Walker, B. 1879a. Notes upon Discoveries made during the recent restoration of Landbeach Church, Cambridge. Antiquarian Communications, XIX, pp.245-259.

Walker, B. 1879b. Cambridge Chronicle, Letter, May 15, 1879.

Walker, B., Rector of Landbeach 1871 - 87. Collectanea de Landbeach. Vol.2. Archives of Corpus Christi College, Cambridge.

RECTORS OF LANDBEACH

1160	Pers de Cantebrigg	1554	William Whalteye B.A.
1216	William Fitzhumfrey	1558	John Poric BA.
1229	William de London	1569/70	Henry Clifford M.A.
1240	Richard de London	1616/17	William Rawley B.A.
1255	Laurence de Mannebye	1667	Francis Wilford D.D.
	Thebaud le Chaumberlyn	1683	William Spencer M.A.
1272	David de Offington	1688	John Cory B.D.
1294	John le Chaumberlyn	1727	John Mickleborough B.D.
1299	Richard de Walpole	1756	Robert Masters B.D.
1308	Thomas de Berningham	1797	Thomas Cooke Borroughs
1323	John de Herdewick	1821	Edward Addison B.D.
1345/6	John de Stowe	1843	John Tinkler B.D., MA., LL.D.
1349	Richard Abbat	1871	Bryan Walker MA., LLD.
1365	John atte Church	1887	William Duguid Stephen B.A.
1374	Thomas de Eltisle LBD	1910	John Fitzstephen Rentino D.D.
1375	Thomas de Eltisle Dec.Bac.	1911	James Thomason Lang M.A.
1376	John Campion BA	1922	Ronald Kynaston Denham M.A.
1379/80	Adam le Leverington B.A.	1948	Frederick A. O. Sanders M.A.
1391	John de Necton D.D.	1960	Brian Frederick Dupre M.A.
1398	Thomas Bodneye MA.	1976	Patrick George Jones *priest-in-charge, also of Waterbeach*
1429	Adam Clerke		
1462	Richard Brocher B.D.		
1488/90	Thomas Cosyn	1979	Peter S.G. Cameron B.D., M.A.
1515	John Seyntwary B.D.	1983	Brian J. Macdonald-Milne M.A.
1516/17	Peter Nobys B.D.	1988	David P.E Reindorp M.A.
1523	John Cuttynos B.D.	1998	Nicholas Ian Moir M.A.
1528	William Sowode B.D.	2008	Lucy Eleanor Cleland B.Sc., B.Th. *priest-in-charge, also of Waterbeach*
1554	Thomas Cobbis M.A.		
1545	Matthew Parker D.D. *consecrated Archbishop of Canterbury 17 December 1559*		

An illuminated list of Rectors from AD 1160 was placed in the church in November 1923, the gift of Mrs Bryan Walker and made by Mr West of Cambridge (Denham, 1923). The updated list now extends to two boards on either side of the south door.

INDEX

INDEX

AUTHOR

Ray Gambell has lived in Landbeach since 1976. He has been Reader since 1979 and Churchwarden from 1992 of All Saints' Church. He oversaw the addition of the new North Porch, heating system and facilities to the church in 2006.

Ray was educated at Reading University, receiving the degree of B.Sc. in Zoology and subsequently a Ph.D. After graduating he worked in fisheries research in Aberdeen for six years. The rest of his professional life was spent as a whale biologist, based first in London and then for 24 years in Cambridge as Secretary to the International Whaling Commission. He was awarded the OBE in the New Year's Honours in 1994 for services to the biology and the conservation of whales.